WRITE NOW

hinkler

Published by Hinkler Books Pty Ltd
45–55 Fairchild Street
Heatherton Victoria 3202 Australia
www.hinkler.com

hinkler

© Hinkler Books Pty Ltd 2019

Author: Ellie Marney
Cover Design: Bianca Zuccolo
Prepress: Splitting Image
Internal Design: Bianca Zuccolo and Emma Pike

Images © Shutterstock.com

ISBN: 978 1 4889 1310 5

Printed and bound in China

WRITING STORY

Imagine, inspire, ignite...

Congratulations! You've taken the first step of your writing journey, which is to pick up your pen and get started. Expressing yourself through writing is a great way to experiment with your creativity – it's good for the soul. Whether you write for publication, to share with friends, or just for yourself, as an activity to get your brain moving by thinking outside the box, creative writing is a wonderful outlet and a great way to inspire and nurture yourself.

Have you got an idea for a story you'd like to write? If you have, then that makes things even easier! But sometimes imagination needs a little help, and the ball takes a while to get rolling. If you're ever stuck on what to write about, there are a few sure-fire techniques you can use to get your imaginative juices flowing...

External resources

These are the things that are all around you. Some of the best stories come from things like: newspaper headlines; music (which creates mood) or music lyrics; overheard conversations; the natural world (walking around in natural environments is always inspiring); other media (film, television shows, podcasts and books); observing people (in cafes, on public transport); photos and pictures; special interest articles; conversations with friends and family; and travel to new places. Potential stories are all around you.

Internal resources

These are the resources you already have inside you. You can find inspiration in personal things like: your own memories; dreams (keep a dream journal beside your bed!); your opinions and ideas about different subjects; your plans and goals for the future; daydreams; your own life experiences. Believe it or not, sometimes being bored is a good way of finding inspiration, because your brain will create something out of nothing to keep itself entertained!

Writing journal

It's always a good idea to keep a writing journal with you at all times. Whether you use it to jot down ideas, capture observations, make notes about a story, write out snippets of dialogue, stick in inspiring pictures and quotes, outline a dream you had, sketch out a scene... Whatever you use it for, a writing journal can be one of a writer's most important tools.

Writing sprints

Time yourself! Set a timer for five minutes, and in that period write whatever you like without stopping. Timed sprints are a good way to brush out the cobwebs and get into the writing flow and usually when the time is up you won't want to stop. Don't think too hard – just write! You can increase the time of each sprint gradually until you find a length of time that suits you.

Picture prompts

Visuals are always inspiring – and easy to access. You can look through old photos or pictures, or search for a particular topic online and view the images that way. Or you can simply wander through online image databases like Pinterest for images that grab your imagination (be careful not to get distracted though!)

Writing prompts

If writing prompts are what you need to fire up, then read on – we have plenty of prompts and exercises for you to try!

STORY STRUCTURE
Finding the write path

While some people prefer to put pen to paper (or fingers to keyboard) with no idea of where the road will lead them, most writers agree that structuring your story is a sensible idea – even if you do it after you've finished writing. Structure helps you fully understand your story and where it's going, and can give you incentive to continue.

Check out these story structure options and find the one that seems to be the best fit for your writing style and subject matter.

Three-Act Structure

This is a very popular type of narrative structure that some people claim was invented by Aristotle, because he noted that a story must have a beginning, a middle and an end. It's still used by many storytellers and screenwriters today. The Three-Act narrative begins with Act One and some early exposition, then a dramatic incident that sends the protagonist into the action. After a series of obstacles and a significant personal turning point, the protagonist will suffer some kind of disaster or crisis before the dramatic climax of the story (e.g. the hero meets the villain in battle). Once remaining challenges are overcome and subplots are resolved, the protagonist's story reaches its conclusion. The middle section of the story, Act Two, is typically longer than both the beginning and the ending, and the arc of the story's tension rises at the opening of Act Three until the climax, then falls as the protagonist reaches the finale. You can see the Three-Act Structure in action in most Marvel superhero films and many other Hollywood blockbusters.

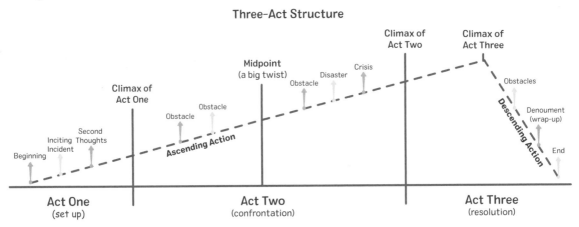

Hero's Journey

The use of archetypes and myth in writing structure was a concept crystallised by Joseph Campbell, who found there to be a clear pattern to satisfying fiction plots: a hero goes on a quest or adventure, wins a victory after a crisis, then comes home altered by his or her experiences. With a title like 'the Hero's Journey' you'd think this structure only applies to epic fantasy stories, but you'd be surprised by how many contemporary stories in other genres follow this same structure. In this structure, the hero receives a call to adventure, and is usually met along their path by some kind of guide or mentor who helps them overcome challenges and temptations. When the hero reaches their lowest point, where everything seems to be going wrong, a revelation will allow them to achieve a transformation, climb out of their despair and fulfil their quest. They are usually given some kind of gift from a goddess-like character upon their return to their known world. You can read the Hero's Journey in action through books including *The Hobbit*, *Lord of the Rings* and *Jane Eyre*, or movies such as *Star Wars: A New Hope* and even *The Lion King*.

Ivy Structure

This is a simple type of structure frequently used by writers of creative non-fiction, modelled on a branch of ivy. The stem of the ivy is the central theme or message of the piece, and each leaf represents a scene, opinion or researched fact. Scenes can come one after another, or be clustered together to create emphasis.

Save the Cat Structure

This is a structure that was originally developed by screenwriter Blake Snyder, as a template for screen-writing narratives. You can use it for fiction, too, especially if your story is highly visual. Modelled somewhat on both the Hero's Journey and Three-Act Structure, the simple idea behind this structure is that you want to stick a cat (your protagonist) up a tree (i.e. in a difficult position) and then throw rocks at them (make their problem even worse).

Save the Cat starts with an opening image of the ordinary world, but the protagonist is soon confronted by a catalyst that spurs them to take action and break into Act Two and take on the challenges ahead. In Act Two, like the plot structures above, the task at hand will all become too much and all will seem lost, but eventually the protagonist will push through to find inspiration for the big finale. Save the Cat structure takes into account story elements like cascading catastrophes (when a character tries to find a solution to a problem but the solution makes things worse) and foreshadowing (for example, if a character puts a gun on the mantle, chances are they'll use it later in the story).

IMPROVING YOUR CRAFT

Everyone has particular areas of skill in daily life – and the same goes for writing life. Some writers have a real affinity for clever, natural-sounding dialogue. Some find that developing great characters is their strength. You might discover that you have a knack for description, while your friend is fantastic at pacing and structure...and so it goes, because everyone is different.

You can use the exercises in this book to develop a more rounded writing style: one that emphasises your strength areas and builds up the areas in which you need a little support. Need to improve your setting and description skills? Try the exercises on Scene Setting. If you're having trouble with your plotting, maybe give the Five Story Elements or the Mind-Mapping exercises a go. If writing characters is your fatal flaw, the Character Dossier or Secondary Character exercises might help – or even the Out-of-Character prompts. Difficulties with dialogue? The Dialogue Kickstarter exercise is made for you. And if you're having trouble getting started, then get your brain moving with a Story Starter or Fill in the Blanks exercise.

In your own writing, you will find that some things come easy and some things don't. But don't give up on them! Professional writers are always working to improve their craft by reading more, checking out writing craft books, asking for tips from other writers and – the most important thing of all – by writing more and more.

STORY STYLE
Pantsing vs plotting and beyond

Writers talk about finding their 'voice' – each writer's unique tone – in their work. They also talk about style, which is more to do with how they set down words on the page. Each writer has their own way, but writers are often defined by two types of process.

Pantsing

A shortened word for 'seat-of-the-pants' writing, or writing without a formal plan or structure in mind. Pantsers prefer to start with a character and an idea and a blank page, and see how things develop naturally. They tend to follow their instincts, and allow the narrative to find its own structure as they write. Pantsers are usually quite character-driven – they like to flesh out the characters in their head, and then set the characters loose on the page. This strategy can create its own difficulties – you may find the empty page daunting at first, and you may need to go back and rewrite sections of your story as the narrative structure takes shape – but the advantages of pantsing are an undeniable creative freedom, plus a deep connection to characters that allows you to follow where they lead.

Plotting

Exactly what it says – writers who plot like to have all the narrative threads figured out before they start putting words on the page. Some plotters write down extensive chapter lists, including details about what will happen in each scene. Others simply start with a plan of the basic plot points and go from there. With this style of writing, you may lose some spontaneity and character connection – the writer is the boss of the story, not the characters – but you gain a deep control of the rhythm and aims of the narrative, and radically reduce the need for rewriting later.

Although most writers are divided into the pantsing v plotting camps, some writers choose to use a combination of both styles for their writing – they start with characters and an idea and a plan for where they'd like the narrative to go.

The most important thing to remember is: your writing style can change, depending on the project. Each story is different – if you plotted out your first story, you might find yourself pantsing more with your second story, or even using a combination of styles. Ultimately you should settle on a style and process that's effective for you and for the project.

THE WRITER'S TOOLBOX

It's easy to work out what a writer's best resource is: words, right?

But there are other resources you have at your fingertips, and you can utilise all the tools in your Writer's Toolbox to make your writing sing.

Thesaurus

The indispensable writer's tool. Whether you have a physical hardcopy version or an online thesaurus, use this regularly to find a richer, more descriptive and specific word than 'nice'.

Dictionary

It's always a good thing to increase your word-power. Improving your vocabulary is going to improve your writing, no doubt. But remember to trust your instincts too – sometimes the first word you think of is the one closest to your real meaning.

Other books

A good writer reads. And reads, and reads, and reads! The best way to improve your vocabulary and develop an awareness of what themes, subjects and characters have already been explored is to read as many books within your preferred genre/s as you can. You will learn a lot about what makes a good book good and a bad book bad.

Five senses

You don't need to simply describe things in your work visually. Always make an effort to stretch your senses into a scene you're writing. Your words should be able to make a reader smell the scents on the breeze, hear the sounds of background action, feel the cool air and taste a good meal on their tongue. Maybe not all at once! A few extra sense-impressions is usually enough – and enough   to show your reader that you're creating something that has depth and texture.

Writing materials

Sounds obvious, but you'd be surprised at the number of writers who've resorted to scrawling things down on napkins! (Or on the back of their hand, or on the reverse of an envelope, or...) Keep a notebook and pencil with you for random inspiration.

SHOW DON'T TELL

The common phrase 'Show Don't Tell' that is often thrown around refers to the writing technique of showing the reader what happens in the story through action, dialogue and feelings, rather than telling the story with exposition and 'info-dumping'.

Have a look at this example of telling:

> Emily watched Garrett pace in front of the window. She was worried about the children, what would happen to them in the overnight cold. From his expression, Garrett didn't seem to have any more idea than she did about how to proceed with the search.

Compared to this example of showing:

> Emily bit her lip. 'So what do you think we should do?'
>
> Garret grimaced at the view out the window. 'It's nearly sundown. If we go back out now we'll never find them in the dark.'
>
> Emily hugged her arms around herself. 'Cleo's only three, Garrett.'
>
> 'I know that.' He worried a thumbnail, staring through the glass.
>
> 'She's never been outside after dark before. She's never even been for a sleepover. And she's only wearing her pyjamas. The police said it'll reach minus-two degrees tonight–'
>
> 'Emily, I know, all right?'

Telling is sometimes necessary, if you need to condense a lot of narrative into a short chapter or section. But showing a character in action, or getting them to speak some dialogue or experience an emotion, is definitely more effective for engaging the reader than explaining things with long internal monologues or descriptions.

POINT OF VIEW
Who's telling this story?

'Point of view' or POV is the perspective through which the story is told, and the voice it's told in. Different points of view create different reader experiences for your story. Here's a handy guide to set you straight:

Are you telling the story as me or I? Then you're writing in First Person. It's one of the most popular points of view to take in fiction. It creates a sense of immediacy, like you're right inside the head of the protagonist and inside the action. Of course, this means that you're limited to what the central character can see, hear, feel and think. But it's a dynamic and intimate perspective for writing, and can be used effectively in everything from junior picture books and YA novels to adult fiction.

Are you writing as he or she or they? Sounds like you're writing in Third Person. This is another frequently used perspective, and comes in three different versions: Third Person Omniscient – when the narrator is all-seeing and all-knowing, which allows the writer to show the thoughts, feelings and actions of a whole cast of characters; Third Person Limited – when the narrative is focused on a single lead protagonist; and finally Deep Third Person – which is so focused on one protagonist that we can see right inside their head, removing things like 'she felt' or 'he wondered' to create a seamless depth of perspective.

Are you writing as you and your? You're probably writing in Second Person. This is a less common perspective to take, and it can be difficult to maintain for a whole novel, but it's a great way to make the reader feel like an active participant in the story. Try it for short stories or literary fiction, and encourage your reader to engage strongly with what's happening in your narrative.

So which point of view are you taking? The main thing is to take one perspective and stick with it, to create consistency for the reader. Go with what feels comfortable to you, and what seems right for the story. You don't need to choose one – you might chose to write from a different perspective in every story you write.

WE LOVE ALL FICTIONAL FORMS

You might want to write a short story that travels in a linear way from A to Z, and that's fantastic.

Or you might want to write a novel the same way – also fantastic!

Or you might want to try piecing your story together non-chronologically. Or you could write an epistolary work, so it's made up of a patchwork of 'found' material, like memos and emails and transcripts. You might like to try your hand at a poem. You might create something intended for performance, like a screen treatment or a script for a theatrical play. If you're a highly visual person and also enjoy drawing, you might like to have a go at writing a graphic novel.

The main thing is that you decide what to write, and in what form you'd like to write it. All forms of fiction are good forms, and the best form is the one that works for you and for the project.

WHAT GENRE IS THAT?

Genre is a categorisation of fiction types, and covers everything from High Literature to High Fantasy, and everything in between. Most genres have their own tropes and codes – themes, subjects, character types and motifs that occur regularly in that particular type of fiction. What would a romance story be without a Happily Ever After? Can you really have a Western without a gunslinger? Or a comedy without jokes? Is a story really a thriller if it's not…well… thrilling?

There are literally dozens of genres (and sub-genres!) in fiction. You can even mash two or more genres together! But remember – if you'd like to write in a genre, it's good to read works of a similar nature. Here are some genres, and a few elements you're likely to see if you read within them:

Romance

A hero and heroine (or a hero/hero, or a heroine/heroine) go on an exploration of their attraction with an emotional journey – often with misunderstandings, personal revelations and spicy kisses – culminating in a Happily Ever After at the finale.

Western

Traditionally set in late 19th century in the American Old West, a Western can be set in any landscape if it includes certain characteristics. Westerns will always be set in a lawless frontier environment (which could even be in outer space!), where hardened characters endure a series of challenges and trials to prove their toughness and self-worth, often forming bonds with unlikely allies.

Paranormal

Ghosts, shapeshifters, vampires, psionic powers…or all of the above can be used to great effect in a strong Hero's Journey structure, where the Chosen One discovers their secret power and then embarks on a voyage of discovery to realise their potential (and find allies and enemies along the way).

Horror

In every location – from haunted houses to deep under the sea – vulnerable characters find their weaknesses exploited in frequently gruesome fashion by monsters of nightmare (while sometimes discovering that the monsters are…people just like them).

Literary

Placing more value on meaning than on entertainment, the characters in these works (which can be set in any location, at any period of time) are well-crafted and real, with evocative language used by the writer to draw out contemporary concerns and themes. Literary works are often introspective, or make larger social commentary through their themes.

Espionage thriller

The high-stakes world of international intelligence operatives is laid bare in these stories of spies and double agents, strike and counter-strike. They are often fast-paced and action-packed with little time for introspection and flowery prose.

Comedy

Can you get a laugh out of any situation? Are pratfalls, gags and silliness the thing you like to write most of all? Can you pen witty snark and clever comebacks? If revealing the funny side of human foibles is what you enjoy most of all, comedy might be for you.

Psychological thriller

Heightened feelings of suspense, anxiety and surprise characterise these stories of individuals experiencing a 'dissolving state of reality' in their lives. Psychological thrillers can veer frighteningly into horror or calm down into gothic mystery, and make for a great genre for readers who enjoy watching a world slightly tilted off its axis.

Action adventure

Characters from all walks of life are thrust into suspenseful and dangerous situations that require explosions, car chases, scuba-diving, cliff-jumping – and more! – to clear their name or save someone (possibly a whole planet). The stakes are high – often life or death – and there is often a time-limit element to enhance tension. Your protagonist must save the day before time runs out!

Police procedural

On the hard, urban streets, or sometimes in the backwater boonies, police detectives search for the tiniest clues hidden in crime scenes in order to bring evil-doers to justice. A police procedural can involve a lot of research into law enforcement in order to get the procedures right.

Science fiction

Deep in the far reaches of space, or maybe on your very own planet sometime in the future, the characters in these stories explore what it means to be human in an ever-changing world.

Cosy mystery

For those who like their dead bodies in the library – and their mysteries wrapped up by tea-time – a non-typical detective like Miss Marple, an every-person not in law enforcement, will take the reader's hand and lead them to the truth about a crime. Though there may be an increasing body count, the tone of a cosy mystery is usually fairly light and easy to read.

Fantasy

In a mythical universe of your own creation, characters with extraordinary powers set forth on a Hero's Journey to vanquish evil and restore order and justice to their magical realm.

WRITE WHAT YOU KNOW?

The oldest writing maxim is 'Write what you know' – but how can you write about being in space if you've never been an astronaut? Or write about deep-sea pearl diving if you've never done it? How can you bring a mermaid or a robot to life if that's (obviously) outside your experience?

First of all, keep in mind that writers research – every writer spends time finding out about a subject (like being in space) in some depth before they plunge into writing about it. And that can be part of the fun! You can usually start by roughing out your ideas, and then when you reach the limit of your understanding, it's time to do some research. You can hit the books or go online to find out facts, and even ask experts for more detail.

The second thing to remember is that you're writing fiction – which means you can make things up. Don't know what it might be like to live on another planet? No problem! No Earthling has ever lived on another planet, so you have absolute licence to imagine whatever details you like. You can even make the planet up from scratch, with details to suit your plot!

The final critical thing to keep in mind is that you actually know a lot already – even if you don't realise it. So your mermaid is having a competitive argument with her mer-sister? Sister relationships might be something you know, so you can surely write about it. Is your robot falling in love? Most of us have had experience with love, so that's the place of understanding you can write from.

'Write what you know' can mean a lot of different things – and with a bit of research and imagination, plus the help of your own life experience and the resources inside you, you can write things that you never dreamed possible.

BRINGING CHARACTERS TO LIFE

A great writer once said that you should never start a story with a description of the weather – and there's a reason for that. Readers are more interested in people than in the weather, which brings us to one of the most important skills of the writer: the ability to bring imagined people to life on the page.

Character development is about adding more and more detail to a character's presentation and backstory until they become indistinguishable from a real person. You might know what your character looks like, but do you know what they had for breakfast? Do you know their family background? Whether they're a heavy or a light sleeper? Their particular skills and talents? Their vices and bad habits and weaknesses? What are their likes – food, music, television, games – and (perhaps more revealing) their dislikes? What would you discuss if you were on a road trip with them? Any and all of these things can have an impact on a character's personality and behaviour.

If you want to write a character well, you have to get down to the meat and bones of their personality and their history. Some writers create detailed character dossiers, with pictures and information on everything from the hair gel their character uses to their terrible relationship with their cousin. Other writers answer long character questionnaires that explore every aspect of their character's lives so that they can really bring them to life.

However you do it, spend some time getting to know your characters – especially your central protagonist. Understanding your character's hair gel preferences might be integral to your story's plot at some point!

SET THE SCENE
Writing settings

Writing is about taking your reader on a journey – and every reader likes to visit new and interesting places! When writing setting and location, you will have a chance to give your description skills free rein.

Setting isn't just about plonking the characters down anywhere, either. There are a number of elements that create a setting: the geography of a place, the weather and climate, the time of year, the buildings and structures, the mood and atmosphere, and the passing of time. You may not need to touch on all of these things, but they make up some of the aspects of setting that a reader might require for a fuller understanding of the environment in which the characters find themselves.

Other things you might like to touch on include the local population of a place, the social, political and cultural influences impacting on the location, any historical events that happened there (particularly if they affect the character who is there now), and the generational influences surrounding the place.

Seems like a lot, doesn't it? You don't have to include all these things – be judicious about the aspects of setting and location that you use. Include the ones that have particular relevance to the characters, but don't spend ten pages on description. Usually a few paragraphs is ample, and then scatter a few others here and there to create mood and awareness. Then set your characters loose to explore their new world.

HE SAID, SHE SAID, THEY ALL SAID...
Writing dialogue

The most important thing to remember about dialogue is that it's not like real speech. There's no 'um's or 'ah's or 'er...'s to contend with. Written dialogue filters out all the little interjections and hesitations that clutter up real speech.

Written dialogue also trims the repetition from most casual speech, and retains only the most critical parts – the parts that reveal character, or push the plot forward, or provide mood and scene details. Done well, dialogue can be one of a writer's most useful tools! You can even write a whole story just in dialogue, as a script. But remember some of the key issues with dialogue to steer your course:

Dialogue must always have a purpose

In real life we chat to pass the time, but every spoken exchange in fiction must help your story along in some way. It might tell us what a character is feeling or thinking, or give us a clue to their personality. It might provide some detail about the setting or location, or evoke a mood in the reader. Or it might even provide some conflict to propel the narrative, or keep us up to date with the events of the story.

Dialogue usually happens as people do other things

In this respect, written dialogue is more like reality. Have your characters performing some kind of action (that's relevant to the scene, of course) as they talk, so their conversation seems natural.

Dialogue tags are useful

Make sure your readers know which character is saying what by using tags like 'he said' and 'she asked', especially if you have an ensemble cast talking together. If it's only a duet dialogue, you can leave out some of the tags to create smoother flow.

Dialogue is best when 'said'

The reason we use 'said' instead of 'screamed' or 'wailed' etc. the majority of the time is because 'said' is invisible: it blends into the background, almost unobserved by the reader. 'Said' is the most effective way of tagging dialogue. You can use adverbs ('she said breathlessly') but do so sparingly as they can become cumbersome and tend to look amateurish. Before throwing in an adverb, check the language in your dialogue to make sure it isn't already expressing the character's tone and delivery.

Dialogue is sometimes left unsaid

Subtext is inferred by the reader from pauses, topic avoidance, hesitant responses or mumbled replies. Remember that sometimes it's not about what's being said in an exchange; what's not being said can be just as powerful.

A WHOLE NEW WORLD...
World-building

You might be creating a high-flying world of international spies, or a wild green jungle of sentient animals, or an alien planet with an alien society – whatever situation your character is in, whatever story you create, it's important that you spend some time considering the world-building aspects.

World-building is more than just setting – it covers every social and environmental condition of the situation your characters find themselves in. What is the code of conduct that your international spies must abide by? What kids or family arrangements do your sentient animals have? Do your aliens have a religion? All these things and more will inform your characters' journey through this world and culture, and you need to know what those things are before you even start writing about them.

Here are a few examples to guide you:

You're writing about a team of super-soldiers sent on a mission

What kinds of uniforms do they wear? What's their command structure? What kinds of rations do they eat while on this mission? What kinds of weapons do they carry? Are they gender-neutral? (i.e. are your soldiers of all different genders?) What kinds of logistical issues might this raise in regards to fraternisation policies? Are they the 'goodies' or the 'baddies'? Do they know if they're the goodies or the baddies?

You're writing about a special envoy to an alien planet

How does your envoy arrive on-planet? Were they expected? What aspects of alien culture does your envoy have to contend with? Language barriers? Cultural intricacies? Social arrangements? Religious issues? Political squabbles? What kinds of food do the aliens eat that your envoy might struggle with? What aspects of this new culture might your envoy have the most trouble dealing with, and why?

You're writing about a group of French resistance fighters

What is the historical period in which the group operated? What are the political and social issues that dominate the cultural environment of that period? What clothes would they wear? What about their shoes? What weapons or tactics would they use?

Prepare a world-building sheet that details as much information as possible, so you don't get confused mid-story. Each aspect must make logical sense – be aware of flow-on effects from one aspect to another. World-building is about creating a whole new world (or researching an old one) for your characters, and investigating every aspect so your characters can blend seamlessly with their environment.

STUMBLING BLOCKS
Breaking through writer's block

We've all been there: you're in the middle of writing a scene or a story, and you start the next sentence and then...you're stuck. The words aren't flowing. Nothing is going right. What do you do?

The main thing you need to remember is that **it happens to everybody** – every writer reaches points in their story where they get stuck or blocked or can't seem to figure out what happens next. You're not alone.

It's also important to keep in mind that **persistence is the key**. The difference between a professional author and a hobby writer is...professional authors finish what they start. Even if it means ploughing through pages of hard-to-write, clunky words that seem to go in circles, professional authors keep going and push to the other side, and then things start to improve.

You also have to know that **first drafts are often bad drafts** – and everything can be improved during editing! Maybe these pages sound forced, and maybe these words aren't the ones you're after, but the important thing is to get the words out of your head and onto the page first. You can fix anything that needs fixing later.

Sometimes you might have trouble because you invented a character, and now you want them to perform certain actions or go in certain directions – but the character has other ideas. If you've created real, three-dimensional people, that's great! But sometimes you'll find that **your characters like to make their own choices** (as silly as that may sound), and they might not be in line with what you had in mind. Be led by your characters, and they'll steer you right.

If you're really struggling, **go back to where your work was flowing** and see what happened. Did you make an authorial choice that has gummed up the flow of the action? Did you choose Path A for your character when they really should have gone along Path B? See if you can figure out where your misstep occurred and change it. It might be that simple to get the words flowing again.

If you're having heaps of trouble and it's making your brain melt, it's no crime to **step away from your work for a while**. Take a break, go for a walk, talk to friends and family, read a book, watch a movie, do some exercise or enjoy another hobby for a while – you'll often find that when you return to your writing, you'll see things more clearly.

WRITE NOW

THE PROMPTS

THE WRITING PROMPTS IN THIS BOOK

Character creator

Don't know the personality of the character you want to write about? Fill in the character profile and suddenly you'll know the person you're wanting to write about, their likes, dislikes, habits, family dynamics, friendships and more a lot more clearly. This technique helps you create characters just as real and complex as in life.

Dialogue kickstarter

Try writing a short story or scene that is all dialogue! It can be surprising just how much of a story can be conveyed simply through characters talking. You can get an idea of the characters and the story taking place just from how they say what they say – or what they choose not to say at all.

Don't think, just write!

Set a timer to write for a short period – ten minutes or less. Quickly read the simple prompt and follow directions for a brain-exercise jolt to get your imagination moving!

Fill in the blank

Choose words to fill in the blanks from the selection provided, or dream up your own. Once you've completed the sentence, continue the story.

Five story elements

Each of the bubbles contains an element for a story. Fill in any empty bubbles, and then combine all five elements to kick off your tale...

Graphic novel

Using the prompt words listed at the top of the page, complete the storyboard for your graphic novel concept. You can use the words as a feature of character dialogue (don't forget speech bubbles!) or incorporate the ideas into your illustrations.

Keyword story

Take the title as your jumping-off point and use as many of the keywords in your scene or story as you can.

Mind-mapping

Complete the mind-map, brainstorming around the central concept in the middle. Add in potential characters, plot points, settings and whatever you can think of. Then outline your story using all your brainstormed ideas from this map. Once you have characters and plot points you'd like to explore, write a story outline or a key scene, using at least one of these ideas.

Out-of-character

Write a scene about a character type in situations you are not used to seeing them in. Using these odd-couple prompts, let your imagination run wild!

Setting the scene

Continue describing the scene or location in the sentence, then explore from there…

Secondary characters

Secondary characters should be just as three-dimensional as lead protagonists! Create the main character's perfect foil – they could be a bosom friend or an arch-nemesis, but in what story would you set these two characters loose? Once you have fleshed out your secondary character, write a scene in which the protagonist and your character interact.

Story starter sentence

Use the opening line and expand it into a whole scene or story – what happens next?

Try a new genre

Try your hand at writing in a variety of genres – you might find you enjoy writing in a genre you never expected to! Here's your chance to play with genre tropes – you can expand on these ideas or flip them. Once you've written your concept outline, write onward.

Using body language

Use these body language cues to write a scenario in which characters interact. You may be prompted with a starting sentence, or you may want to let your imagination free.

World-building

Read the description of the scenario and then follow the prompt to think about what this world would be like and add crucial world-building detail to your story.

'Better to write
for yourself and have
no public, than to write
for the public and
have no self.'

CYRIL CONNOLLY

STORY STARTER SENTENCE

Continue the story.

They tracked her for nine hours by following the blood on the snow... _____

_____

_____

_____

_____

_____

_____

_____

_____

_____

_____

_____

_____

_____

_____

_____

_____

_____

_____

_____

_____

_____

_____

_____

_____

_____

_____

_____

_____

_____

WORLD-BUILDING

What would this world be like? What impact would it have on the plot and your characters?
Write your story.

Captain Kel Diamond has crash-landed on an alien planet with a rich oxygen content that is bursting with green life. Kel is rescued by a family of local inhabitants. *Describe the home of the family that rescues Kel in as much detail as possible.*

_____

_____

_____

_____

_____

_____

_____

_____

_____

_____

_____

_____

_____

_____

_____

_____

_____

_____

_____

_____

_____

_____

_____

_____

_____

_____

_____

_____

_____

_____

CHARACTER CREATOR

NAME Aldo Green

OCCUPATION Taxi driver

AGE 42 years old

SPECIAL SKILLS Driving under pressure (former getaway driver); hot-wiring cars; engine repair; mental map of all city streets

FRIENDS Larry, a former ventriloquist; Ace, a Muay-Thai kickboxer; Billy, a Maltese-Shih tzu cross

PHYSICAL DESCRIPTION Average height, heavy build, wears undershirts beneath button-down shirts and taxi company trousers; a bit of a slob; three-day growth of whiskers

LIVES IN A run-down bachelor apartment that he tries to brighten up with small pots of daisies

HOW THEY FEEL ABOUT WHERE THEY LIVE He would like to move into a nicer place, but he can't afford to...unless he takes illegal work

FAVOURITE FOOD Onion rings from the place around the corner

LEAST FAVOURITE FOOD Salad

VICES Fast-food addict; not always the best judge of character; has good intentions but not always on the right side of the law

MOST SIGNIFICANT CHILDHOOD MEMORY Playing with toy cars in his grandfather's auto-repair shop

HANDLES BOREDOM BY Talking to Billy; playing games on his phone; eating; reading the newspaper (sports and the classifieds. He's always after a bargain); listening to radio sports; tinkering on cars

DEALS WITH FRUSTRATION BY Kicking tyres, raising his voice; complaining to Larry and Ace

Now that you know your character, it's time to write about them.

Aldo is a nice guy: not particularly bright but with a certain level of street smarts, and a basically sunny disposition. When he's contacted by a local mafia thug and forced to agree to check out the house of a wealthy heiress, he...

_____

_____

_____

_____

_____

_____

_____

_____

_____

_____

_____

_____

_____

_____

_____

_____

_____

_____

_____

_____

_____

_____

_____

_____

_____

_____

_____

_____

_____

_____

FILL IN THE BLANK

Fill in the blanks and write the story.

'It's_____.'

'So? That doesn't mean I have to _____ right now.'

| time | Tuesday | them | / | lie | think | talk |

_____

_____

_____

_____

_____

_____

_____

_____

_____

_____

_____

_____

_____

_____

_____

_____

_____

_____

_____

_____

_____

_____

_____

_____

_____

SETTING THE SCENE

Where does this story take place? Describe the setting as you tell the story.

Once the blindfold was removed, Lin took in her surroundings in a series of quick glances. She saw...

_____

_____

_____

_____

_____

_____

_____

_____

_____

_____

_____

_____

_____

_____

_____

_____

_____

_____

_____

_____

_____

_____

_____

_____

_____

_____

_____

_____

_____

_____

KEYWORD STORY

Include these words to write the story A Candlelit Dinner Goes Awry.

| aroma | romance | choice | carpet | nauseous |
| roses | ocean | stumble | portion | watch |

A Candlelit Dinner Goes Awry

OUT-OF-CHARACTER

Write a story about a character type you know, in a situation you're not used to seeing them in.

The world's deadliest assassin is brought low by...a head cold. But what happens when the ailing assassin gets a phone call for a new job?

_____
_____
_____
_____
_____
_____
_____
_____
_____
_____
_____
_____
_____
_____
_____
_____
_____
_____
_____
_____
_____
_____
_____
_____
_____
_____
_____
_____
_____

TRY A NEW GENRE

Have you ever written a story in this genre? Here's your chance to try something you're unfamiliar with.

ROMANCE: You are the lowly office administration assistant in a large law firm, until one day your gorgeous boss makes a terrible error on an all-staff memo, which you catch just in time. In gratitude for your heart-stopping save, your boss offers to do three favours of your choosing, redeemable at any time...

_____

_____

_____

_____

_____

_____

_____

_____

_____

_____

_____

_____

_____

_____

_____

_____

_____

_____

_____

_____

_____

_____

_____

_____

_____

_____

_____

_____

_____

DON'T THINK, JUST WRITE!

Don't stop writing until you reach the bottom of the page!

Describe these colours as if they were people:

red   yellow   green   blue   violet   black

_____
_____
_____
_____
_____
_____
_____
_____
_____
_____
_____
_____
_____
_____
_____
_____
_____
_____
_____
_____
_____
_____
_____
_____
_____
_____
_____
_____
_____

WORLD-BUILDING

What would this world be like? What impact would it have on the plot and your characters?
Write your story.

Your protagonist is the leader of a small band of children who have been abandoned in the desert as a sacrifice to a horrifying blood spirit. When the children trek across the desert to escape, what environmental conditions do they contend with?

_____

_____

_____

_____

_____

_____

_____

_____

_____

_____

_____

_____

_____

_____

_____

_____

_____

_____

_____

_____

_____

_____

_____

_____

_____

_____

DIALOGUE KICKSTARTER

Write a story through dialogue alone. You can get across more than you think!

'Listen – we don't have much time. They're sending me to the quarantine centre.'

'Maybe...Maybe you *should* go.'

'...Are you serious?'

'Look at your arm! Stop trying to hide it. I know you're infected.'

'...
_____
_____
_____
_____
_____
_____
_____
_____
_____
_____
_____
_____
_____
_____
_____
_____
_____
_____
_____
_____
_____
_____
_____
_____
_____

MIND MAPPING

Use a mind map to plot a story, then write it.

Experienced detective plus younger partner - maybe partner knows area?

Police Experts
· Investigators
· Photographers
· Plain clothes
· Uniform
· Forensics

Victim/s
· Who?
· Possible motive?

Crime Scene

Witnesses
· Are there any?
· Who?

C.O.D (Cause of Death)
· Lots of blood
· Misleading evidence

Violent Crime Unit
· Possibly ensemble cast?
· They might have trouble with resources in a country setting...

Chain of Command
· Who is in charge?
· Detective reports to...

More than one death - what's the pattern?

Location
· Not city - a country crime
· Smaller pool of suspects?
· Detective might be a fish out of water?

'Inspiration is
everywhere.
Carry a notebook.'

VICTOR
HUGO

STORY STARTER SENTENCE

Continue the story.

There was nothing in the guidebook about this – she checked twice. But there it was, right in

front of her... _____

_____

_____

_____

_____

_____

_____

_____

_____

_____

_____

_____

_____

_____

_____

_____

_____

_____

_____

_____

_____

_____

_____

_____

_____

_____

_____

_____

_____

OUT-OF-CHARACTER

Write a story about a character type you know, in a situation you're not used to seeing them in.

A family's pet budgerigar becomes the key to saving them all from a terrible accident. How does this happen?

_____

_____

_____

_____

_____

_____

_____

_____

_____

_____

_____

_____

_____

_____

_____

_____

_____

_____

_____

_____

_____

_____

_____

_____

_____

_____

SECONDARY CHARACTERS

PROTAGONIST — A quiet librarian with a clever mind, who enjoys watching action movies and always has a book quote handy.

SECONDARY CHARACTER — The librarian's best friend and sidekick, Beatrice Plum.

PHYSICAL DESCRIPTION — Beatrice is willowy and beautiful. She is also colour-blind, horrifically clumsy and very near-sighted. She wears overalls with lots of pockets, hand-knitted jumpers with ugly decorations, black lace-up boots and enormous glasses with thick lenses. She always carries a handkerchief.

PERSONALITY — Rather than being daunted by her lack of coordination, Beatrice is quite fearless. She marches straight into any situation without worrying too much about the consequences. Courageous and plain-speaking, she can also be a bit impatient, and doesn't put up with those who lie or manipulate, or are indecisive. She is generally optimistic, and enjoys good food and brandy.

BACKSTORY — Beatrice is the youngest child of a large family, which is how she acquired her no-nonsense confidence and pragmatism – she's always had to stick up for herself...

Write a scene in which the protagonist and the secondary character interact.

_____
_____
_____
_____
_____
_____
_____
_____
_____
_____
_____
_____
_____
_____
_____
_____
_____
_____

GRAPHIC NOVEL

Use the words below in dialogue or in your drawings to create the graphic novel Mean Streets.

Mean Streets

windswept   drizzle   street   litter   grey

sign   overhead   huddle   concrete   streetlamp

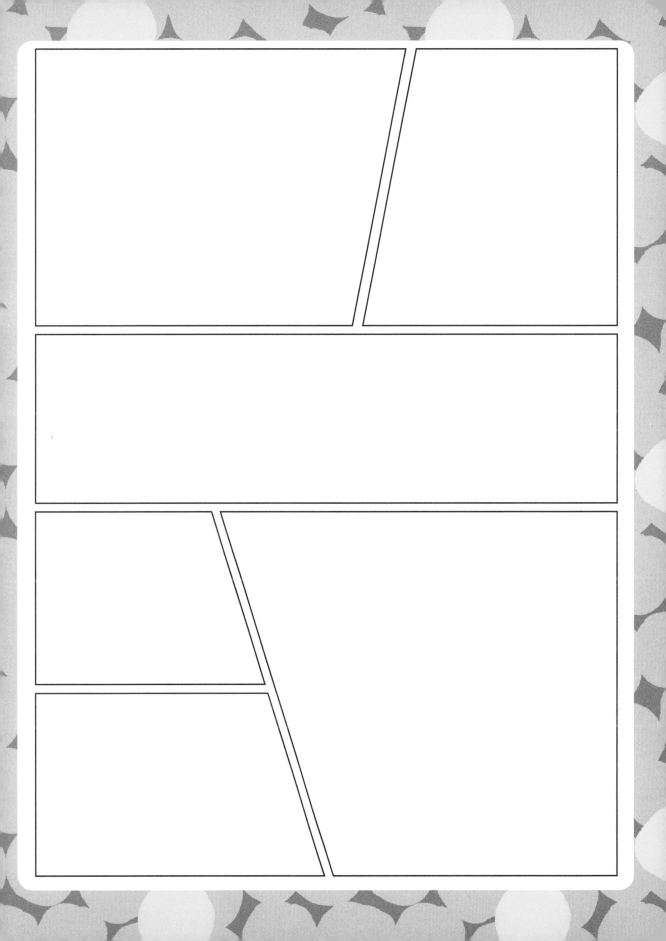

KEYWORD STORY

Include these words to write the story Accidental Superhero.

costume	mysterious	note	texture	vision
nonsensical	believe	reluctant	fly	villain

Accidental Superhero

_____

_____

_____

_____

_____

_____

_____

_____

_____

_____

_____

_____

_____

_____

_____

_____

_____

_____

_____

_____

_____

_____

_____

_____

_____

_____

SETTING THE SCENE

Where does this story take place? Describe the setting as you tell the story.

This wasn't country he was familiar with. The hills shot up like knives and the air was crisp... _____

_____

_____

_____

_____

_____

_____

_____

_____

_____

_____

_____

_____

_____

_____

_____

_____

_____

_____

_____

_____

_____

_____

_____

_____

_____

_____

_____

_____

FIVE STORY ELEMENTS

Create the missing story element and write the story.

SITUATION A girl lives and works as a scullery maid in a castle. Her brother – transformed into a fox by an evil spell – lives in the forest nearby.

CHARACTER A scullery maid with bright red hair.

OPPONENT _____
_____

GOAL
- Free the fox brother of his curse.
- Elevate the girl's status.
- Ensure the opponent gets his comeuppance.

OBSTACLE
- The fox spell can only be broken by the witch who cast it but she's nowhere to be found.
- The girl can only visit her brother in secret.
- The king's vizier is organising a fox hunt.

_____
_____
_____
_____
_____
_____
_____
_____
_____
_____
_____
_____
_____

USING BODY LANGUAGE

Use body language cues to write the story and get across how your character feels.

ANGER is a usually an instinctive reaction to a threat – sometimes with an underlying fear of being hurt. The nervous system causes the heart rate to increase, the pupils to dilate, and blood to rise in the face. Some other body language responses include: balled fists, crossed arms, clenched teeth or jaw, shaking the head, trembling in the body, pointing fingers, frowning, flushed cheeks, stamping feet, or a raised voice.

Bonnie stalked into the room, slamming the door behind her. She whirled around... _____

_____

_____

_____

_____

_____

_____

_____

_____

_____

_____

_____

_____

_____

_____

_____

_____

_____

_____

_____

_____

_____

_____

_____

_____

_____

_____

'If you want to
change the world,
pick up your pen
and write.'

MARTIN
LUTHER

TRY A NEW GENRE

Have you ever written a story in this genre? Here's your chance to try something you're unfamiliar with.

WESTERN: The saloon poker match is typical for a Monday night – Drew has folded, Patty is aces-high, and Foggart is drunk. Then in walks this girl who can't be more than twelve years old, in pin-curls and britches, and she asks to join the game...

_____

_____

_____

_____

_____

_____

_____

_____

_____

_____

_____

_____

_____

_____

_____

_____

_____

_____

_____

_____

_____

_____

_____

_____

_____

_____

_____

_____

_____

_____

_____

_____

CHARACTER CREATOR

NAME _____

OCCUPATION _____

AGE _____

SPECIAL SKILLS _____
_____

FRIENDS _____

PHYSICAL DESCRIPTION _____
_____

LIVES IN _____
_____

HOW THEY FEEL ABOUT
WHERE THEY LIVE _____
_____

FAVOURITE FOOD _____

LEAST FAVOURITE FOOD _____

VICES _____
_____

MOST SIGNIFICANT
CHILDHOOD MEMORY _____
_____

HANDLES BOREDOM BY _____
_____

DEALS WITH
FRUSTRATION BY _____
_____

Now that you know your character, it's time to write about them.

Write a story through dialogue alone. You can get across more than you think!

'Hey, just relax, it's okay, you're doing great, I've got you.'

'Don't let me fall – you can't let me fall!'

'I won't let you fall, all right? Ow, your fingers... Stop looking down! Everything's fine, just hold onto me.'

'..._____

_____

_____

_____

_____

_____

_____

_____

_____

_____

_____

_____

_____

_____

_____

_____

_____

_____

_____

_____

_____

_____

FILL IN THE BLANK

Fill in the blanks and write the story.

The _____ rose up, forbidding and brutal, and it was as if it had been waiting for me...

cliff   ogre   frost   noise

_____

_____

_____

_____

_____

_____

_____

_____

_____

_____

_____

_____

_____

_____

_____

_____

_____

_____

_____

_____

_____

_____

_____

_____

_____

_____

_____

_____

_____

_____

DON'T THINK, JUST WRITE!

Write down your favourite story cliché and why you like it.

_____

_____

_____

_____

_____

_____

_____

_____

_____

_____

_____

_____

_____

_____

_____

_____

_____

_____

_____

_____

_____

_____

_____

_____

_____

_____

_____

_____

_____

_____

GRAPHIC NOVEL

Use the words below in dialogue or in your drawings to create the graphic novel Lost in the Wilderness.

Lost in the Wilderness

fronds	green	damp	mud	itchy
footprint	sting	sweat	shirt	birdsong

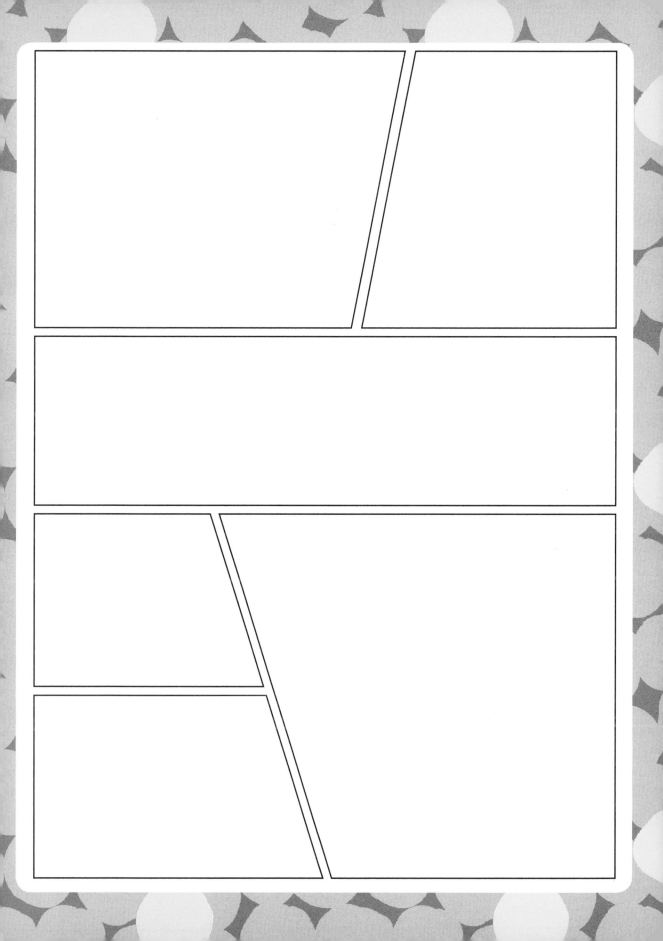

MIND MAPPING

Use a mind map to plot a story, then write it.

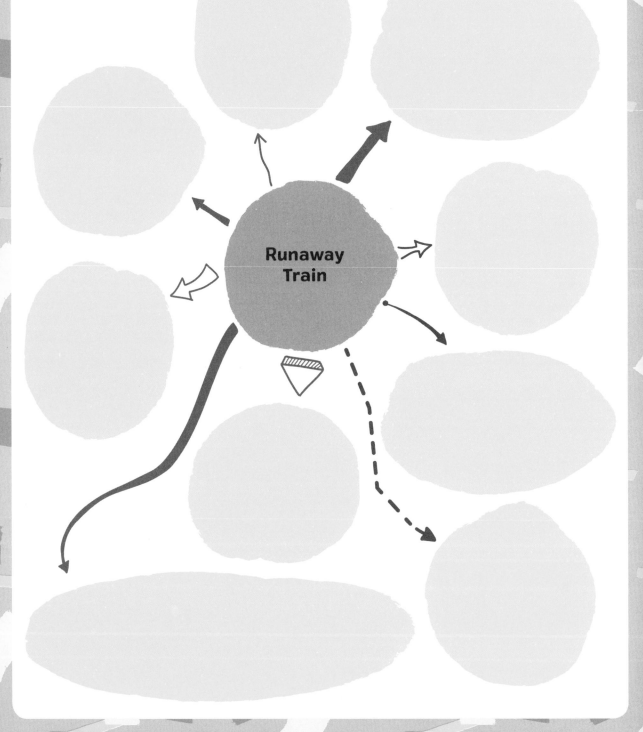

WORLD-BUILDING

What would this world be like? What impact would it have on the plot and your characters? Write your story.

Your story is set on a spaceship, where a group of civilians and military personnel are on the long trip to a mining planet. What do they eat on board, and what is the relationship like between the civilians and their military escorts?

_____

_____

_____

_____

_____

_____

_____

_____

_____

_____

_____

_____

_____

_____

_____

_____

_____

_____

_____

_____

_____

_____

_____

_____

_____

_____

_____

_____

_____

OUT-OF-CHARACTER

Write a story about a character type you know, in a situation you're not used to seeing them in.

Nobody goes into the 'witch's house' on Bleeker Street – until the local plumber is called one day to deal with a blocked toilet. When the plumber enters the house, what do they find?

_____

_____

_____

_____

_____

_____

_____

_____

_____

_____

_____

_____

_____

_____

_____

_____

_____

_____

_____

_____

_____

_____

_____

_____

_____

_____

_____

_____

SECONDARY CHARACTERS

PROTAGONIST — A dedicated gymnast who is heading for Olympic glory.

SECONDARY
CHARACTER
_____
_____

PHYSICAL
DESCRIPTION
_____
_____
_____
_____

PERSONALITY
_____
_____
_____
_____
_____

BACKSTORY
_____
_____
_____
_____
_____
_____
_____
_____

Write a scene in which the protagonist and your secondary character interact.

_____
_____
_____
_____
_____
_____
_____
_____

FIVE STORY ELEMENTS

Create the missing story element and write the story.

SITUATION A spaceship is infected by an airborne disease that transforms people into disfigured zombies.

CHARACTERS A mechanic who knows the schematics of the ship. A scientist who understands the disease.

OPPONENT The ship's captain, who has been infected.

GOAL _____

_____

OBSTACLE · The ship's captain wants to dock at a nearby planet.
· The mechanic and the scientist are personality opposites.
· They only have one undamaged spacesuit.

_____
_____
_____
_____
_____
_____
_____
_____
_____
_____
_____
_____
_____
_____
_____

SETTING THE SCENE

Where does this story take place? Describe the setting as you tell the story.

The room was black; she extended a hand for the switch, but the light didn't come on. She reached

into the darkness and her fingers landed on... _____

_____

_____

_____

_____

_____

_____

_____

_____

_____

_____

_____

_____

_____

_____

_____

_____

_____

_____

_____

_____

_____

_____

_____

_____

_____

_____

_____

_____

_____

_____

KEYWORD STORY

Include these words to write the story Vikings in Love.

| axe | training | flowers | ice | careful |
| hot | battle | delicious | frolic | sail |

Vikings in Love

_____

_____

_____

_____

_____

_____

_____

_____

_____

_____

_____

_____

_____

_____

_____

_____

_____

_____

_____

_____

_____

_____

_____

_____

_____

_____

TRY A NEW GENRE

Have you ever written a story in this genre? Here's your chance to try something you're unfamiliar with.

SCIENCE FICTION: You're chopping vegetables for dinner when the knife slips and slices the back of your hand – but instead of blood and bone, you see metal...

_____

_____

_____

_____

_____

_____

_____

_____

_____

_____

_____

_____

_____

_____

_____

_____

_____

_____

_____

_____

_____

_____

_____

_____

_____

_____

_____

_____

_____

USING BODY LANGUAGE

Use body language cues to write the story and get across how your character feels.

HAPPINESS is a psychological state of wellbeing, with positive or pleasant emotions that range from contentment to pure joy. Happy people exhibit more open body language cues, including: smiling, relaxed posture, broader gestures, wide sparkling eyes, laughter, increased facial micro-expression, grinning and giggling, loose hand movements, maintaining eye contact, or humming.

_____
_____
_____
_____
_____
_____
_____
_____
_____
_____
_____
_____
_____
_____
_____
_____
_____
_____
_____
_____
_____
_____
_____
_____
_____
_____
_____
_____

'The beginning is
always today.'

MARY
WOLLSTONECRAFT

FILL IN THE BLANK

Fill in the blanks and write the story.

He looked like a _____, and there was nothing she could do to stop her reaction...

mess   dream   god   nightmare

_____

_____

_____

_____

_____

_____

_____

_____

_____

_____

_____

_____

_____

_____

_____

_____

_____

_____

_____

_____

_____

_____

_____

_____

_____

_____

_____

_____

STORY STARTER SENTENCE

Continue the story.

When Simon woke up, his hospital room was dark, and smelled bad... _____

_____

_____

_____

_____

_____

_____

_____

_____

_____

_____

_____

_____

_____

_____

_____

_____

_____

_____

_____

_____

_____

_____

_____

_____

_____

_____

_____

_____

GRAPHIC NOVEL

Use the words below in dialogue or in your drawings to create the graphic novel Paris Sewer System.

Paris Sewer System

hollow   footfalls   glistening   dream   luminescence

stench   shadow   stone   grotty   trickle

SECONDARY CHARACTERS

PROTAGONIST   A naïve young king who has been suddenly thrust into power in a warring city.

SECONDARY CHARACTER
_____
_____

PHYSICAL DESCRIPTION
_____
_____
_____
_____

PERSONALITY
_____
_____
_____
_____
_____

BACKSTORY
_____
_____
_____
_____
_____
_____
_____
_____
_____

Fill in the secondary character profile then write a scene in which the protagonist and your secondary character interact.

_____
_____
_____
_____
_____
_____

OUT-OF-CHARACTER

Write a story about a character type you know, in a situation you're not used to seeing them in.

A mermaid discovers that she is short-sighted and needs glasses. How does she find out and how does she manage?

_____

_____

_____

_____

_____

_____

_____

_____

_____

_____

_____

_____

_____

_____

_____

_____

_____

_____

_____

_____

_____

_____

_____

_____

_____

_____

_____

_____

_____

_____

FILL IN THE BLANK

Fill in the blanks and write the story.

Then they drew back the sheet. It's quite possible that I've never been as _____ as I was in that moment...

awestruck   joyful   relieved   horrified

_____

_____

_____

_____

_____

_____

_____

_____

_____

_____

_____

_____

_____

_____

_____

_____

_____

_____

_____

_____

_____

_____

_____

_____

DIALOGUE KICKSTARTER

Write a story through dialogue alone. You can get across more than you think!

'Well, we understand that she punched another student. I'm afraid that behaviour-'

'How do you know that she was the one who started it?'

'Look at-'

'Her hands were like that before. Admit it. You don't really know what happened.'

'...

MIND MAPPING

Use a mind map to plot a story, then write it.

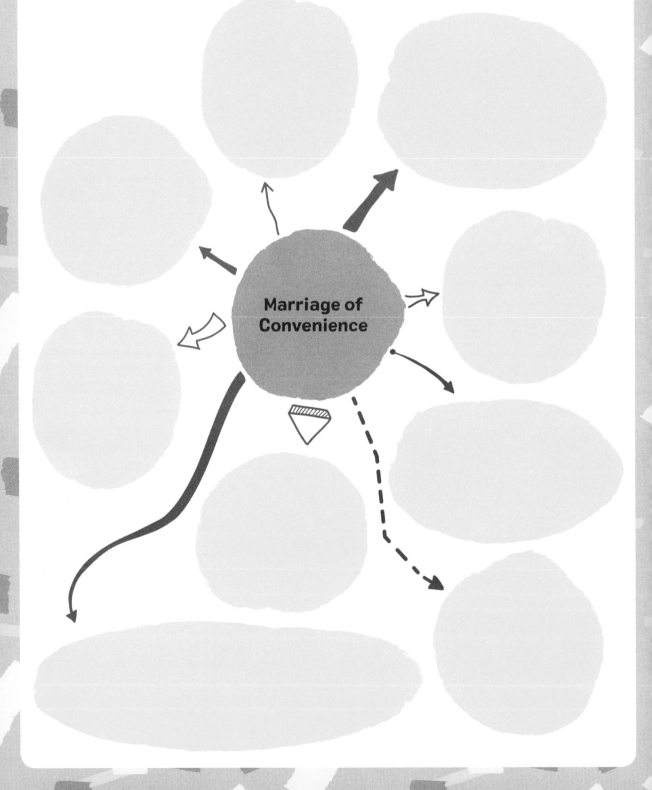

Marriage of Convenience

SETTING THE SCENE

Where does this story take place? Describe the setting as you tell the story.

Warm all over: that's how I felt, standing here. The windows streamed with light and heat... _____

_____

_____

_____

_____

_____

_____

_____

_____

_____

_____

_____

_____

_____

_____

_____

_____

_____

_____

_____

_____

_____

_____

_____

_____

_____

_____

_____

_____

WORLD-BUILDING

What would this world be like? What impact would it have on the plot and your characters? Write your story.

Miss Peggy Entwhistle is the proprietor of a pub in an English village, and the person with the most likely chance of working out who killed the local vicar. Describe four of the village inhabitants she sees as regulars, and their social relationships with each other.

_____
_____
_____
_____
_____
_____
_____
_____
_____
_____
_____
_____
_____
_____
_____
_____
_____
_____
_____
_____
_____
_____
_____
_____
_____
_____
_____
_____
_____
_____

TRY A NEW GENRE

Have you ever written a story in this genre? Here's your chance to try something you're unfamiliar with.

FANTASY: A queen stands in the village square, surrounded by courtiers and villagers, pronouncing a sentence of death on her own son. But as the boy is led to the executioner's block, the queen bursts into flames...

_____

_____

_____

_____

_____

_____

_____

_____

_____

_____

_____

_____

_____

_____

_____

_____

_____

_____

_____

_____

_____

_____

_____

_____

_____

_____

FIVE STORY ELEMENTS

Create the missing story element and write the story.

SITUATION   A member of the royal family in Regency London falls ill. An apothecary's apprentice believes it could be a case of poisoning.

CHARACTER   An apprentice to London's most popular apothecary.

OPPONENT   The old-fashioned conservative doctor to the royal family. A detective from Scotland Yard who refuses to investigate.

GOAL   · Convince the detective.
· Save the victim.
· Solve the case.

OBSTACLE _____

_____

_____

_____

_____

_____

_____

_____

_____

_____

_____

_____

_____

_____

_____

_____

_____

_____

_____

STORY STARTER SENTENCE

Continue the story.

It's late afternoon, and the ground outside the cabin is covered with snow. But you have no choice:

if you don't saddle your horse and leave now, they'll find you... _____

_____

_____

_____

_____

_____

_____

_____

_____

_____

_____

_____

_____

_____

_____

_____

_____

_____

_____

_____

_____

_____

_____

_____

_____

_____

_____

_____

KEYWORD STORY

Include these words to write the story Touchdown.

paint	spiral	win	running	practise
awful	game	cautious	green	helmet

Touchdown

_____

_____

_____

_____

_____

_____

_____

_____

_____

_____

_____

_____

_____

_____

_____

_____

_____

_____

_____

_____

_____

_____

_____

_____

_____

CHARACTER CREATOR

NAME _____

OCCUPATION _____

AGE _____

SPECIAL SKILLS _____
_____

FRIENDS _____

PHYSICAL DESCRIPTION _____
_____

LIVES IN _____
_____

HOW THEY FEEL ABOUT
WHERE THEY LIVE _____
_____

FAVOURITE FOOD _____

LEAST FAVOURITE FOOD _____

VICES _____
_____

MOST SIGNIFICANT
CHILDHOOD MEMORY _____
_____

HANDLES BOREDOM BY _____
_____

DEALS WITH
FRUSTRATION BY _____
_____

Now that you know your character, it's time to write about them.

_____

_____

_____

_____

_____

_____

_____

_____

_____

_____

_____

_____

_____

_____

_____

_____

_____

_____

_____

_____

_____

_____

_____

_____

_____

_____

_____

_____

_____

_____

_____

_____

_____

USING BODY LANGUAGE

Use body language cues to write the story and get across how your character feels.

ATTRACTION is an indication of an interest in or desire for another person, most commonly associated with romantic desire. The physical symptoms of attraction involve: increased heart rate, increases in blood pressure and core body temperature, increased skin sensitivity and heightened emotional response. Body language cues include: flushed cheeks and skin, dilated pupils, deepened voice, leaning forward, physical mirroring (where one person unconsciously copies the movements of the other), steady eye contact, repeated light touching of the other person, staring at erogenous zones (eyes, mouth, etc.), parted lips, or quickened breathing.

_____
_____
_____
_____
_____
_____
_____
_____
_____
_____
_____
_____
_____
_____
_____
_____
_____
_____
_____
_____
_____
_____
_____
_____
_____

'You fail only if you
stop writing.'

RAY
BRADBURY

FILL IN THE BLANK

Fill in the blanks and write the story.

'Hey, take it easy.'

'Don't tell me to take it easy! Would you be able to take it easy, if your _____ was _____?'

mother   boyfriend   psychologist / dead   evil   missing   gorgeous

_____

_____

_____

_____

_____

_____

_____

_____

_____

_____

_____

_____

_____

_____

_____

_____

_____

_____

_____

_____

_____

_____

_____

_____

_____

_____

_____

DON'T THINK, JUST WRITE!

Write down your favourite story cliché and why you like it.

List all your areas of expertise – everything from baking biscuits to understanding vampire lore - and consider how you might incorporate those pieces of knowledge together into a story.

_____

_____

_____

_____

_____

_____

_____

_____

_____

_____

_____

_____

_____

_____

_____

_____

_____

_____

_____

_____

_____

_____

_____

_____

_____

_____

_____

_____

GRAPHIC NOVEL

Use the words below in dialogue or in your drawings to create the graphic novel A Desert Planet.

A Desert Planet

spacesuit · oxygen · light · intense · thirsty

sand · orange · suns · creature · sleep

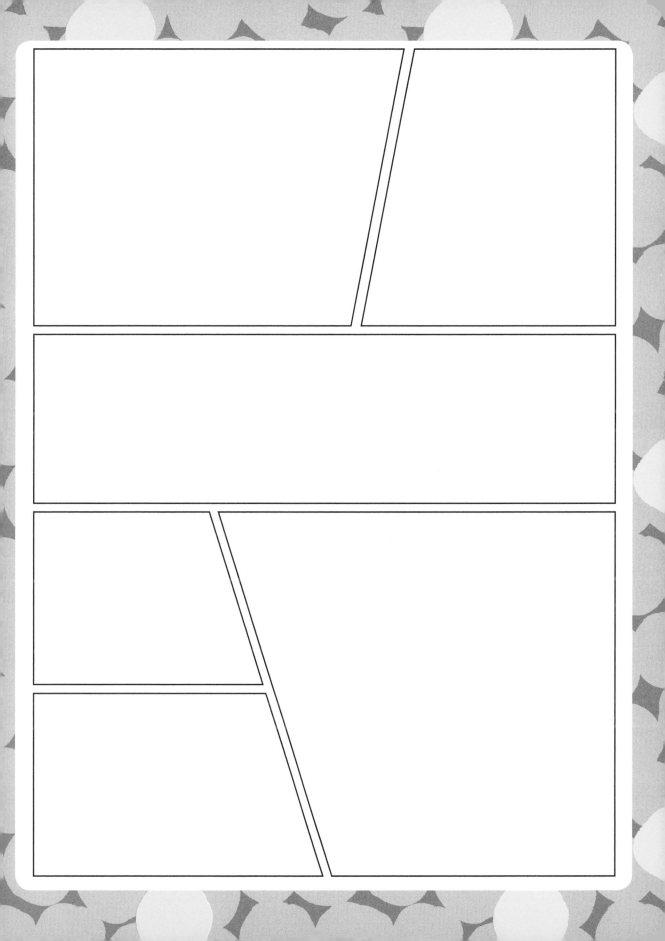

TRY A NEW GENRE

Have you ever written a story in this genre? Here's your chance to try something you're unfamiliar with.

CRIME-NOIR: You're having a whiskey in your office when a beautiful woman walks in and asks you to take on a case. Someone is sending her envelopes that are empty except for a single lock of hair, and she doesn't know why...

_____

_____

_____

_____

_____

_____

_____

_____

_____

_____

_____

_____

_____

_____

_____

_____

_____

_____

_____

_____

_____

_____

_____

_____

_____

_____

_____

_____

SETTING THE SCENE

Where does this story take place? Describe the setting as you tell the story.

It was a private beach. He unlaced his shoes, peeled off his socks, took it all in... _____

_____

_____

_____

_____

_____

_____

_____

_____

_____

_____

_____

_____

_____

_____

_____

_____

_____

_____

_____

_____

_____

_____

_____

_____

_____

_____

_____

_____

_____

_____

_____

_____

STORY STARTER SENTENCE

Continue the story.

We should have been more careful... _____
_____
_____
_____
_____
_____
_____
_____
_____
_____
_____
_____
_____
_____
_____
_____
_____
_____
_____
_____
_____
_____
_____
_____
_____
_____
_____
_____

SECONDARY CHARACTERS

PROTAGONIST   The owner of a pawn shop who is dealing with a crew of thugs in the local area.

SECONDARY CHARACTER _____

_____

PHYSICAL DESCRIPTION _____

_____

_____

_____

PERSONALITY _____

_____

_____

_____

_____

BACKSTORY _____

_____

_____

_____

_____

_____

_____

_____

_____

Fill in the secondary character profile then write a scene in which the protagonist and your secondary character interact.

_____

_____

_____

_____

_____

_____

Use a mind map to plot a story, then write it.

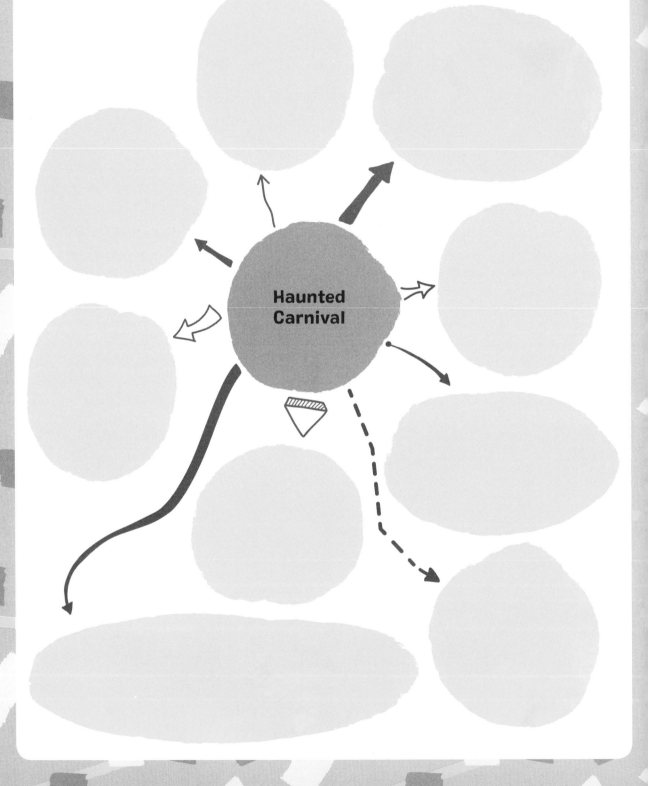

'I declare after all
there is no enjoyment
like reading!'

JANE
AUSTEN

KEYWORD STORY

Include these words to write the story Vicious Spring.

daisy	heat	tendril	meander	painful
stone	bubble	stalk	meat	swallow

Vicious Spring

_____

_____

_____

_____

_____

_____

_____

_____

_____

_____

_____

_____

_____

_____

_____

_____

_____

_____

_____

_____

_____

_____

_____

_____

_____

WORLD-BUILDING

What would this world be like? What impact would it have on the plot and your characters?
Write your story.

Your cast of characters lives and works in a travelling circus. Explain which characters do which jobs when they travel from place to place, and describe the vehicles that get them around.

_____

_____

_____

_____

_____

_____

_____

_____

_____

_____

_____

_____

_____

_____

_____

_____

_____

_____

_____

_____

_____

_____

_____

_____

_____

_____

_____

_____

_____

_____

_____

_____

_____

FIVE STORY ELEMENTS

Create the missing story elements and write the story.

SITUATION   A woman travels by train to find a man she believes is her father after receiving a parcel of mysterious letters.

CHARACTER   _____

_____

OPPONENT   _____

_____

GOAL   · Find out who sent the letters.
· Draw on the woman's courage and intelligence during the journey.
· Bring her to a better understanding of her family and herself.

OBSTACLE   · The train breaks down mid-journey, and the woman must find her way by a variety of means. Another character misleads her.

_____
_____
_____
_____
_____
_____
_____
_____
_____
_____
_____
_____
_____
_____
_____
_____

GRAPHIC NOVEL

Use the words below in dialogue or in your drawings to create the graphic novel High-school Heartache.

High-school Heartache

class	notebook	skirt	fence	smell
corridor	sarcastic	headphones	ignore	crush

FILL IN THE BLANK

Fill in the blanks and write the story.

I wouldn't have described her as _____. She was more _____ than that...

beautiful   funny   malicious   volatile   organised   intelligent   scary

_____
_____
_____
_____
_____
_____
_____
_____
_____
_____
_____
_____
_____
_____
_____
_____
_____
_____
_____
_____
_____
_____
_____
_____
_____
_____
_____
_____

STORY STARTER SENTENCE

Continue the story.

Families are a pain, even when you're the Chosen One. My mother says that after that last stunt, she'll ground me if... _____

_____

_____

_____

_____

_____

_____

_____

_____

_____

_____

_____

_____

_____

_____

_____

_____

_____

_____

_____

_____

_____

_____

_____

_____

_____

_____

_____

_____

TRY A NEW GENRE

Have you ever written a story in this genre? Here's your chance to try something you're unfamiliar with.

ESPIONAGE THRILLER: They say I'm a traitor, and maybe I am, but if I hadn't assassinated the delegate, we would all be dead by now...

_____
_____
_____
_____
_____
_____
_____
_____
_____
_____
_____
_____
_____
_____
_____
_____
_____
_____
_____
_____
_____
_____
_____
_____
_____
_____
_____
_____
_____
_____
_____
_____
_____

USING BODY LANGUAGE

Use body language cues to write the story and get across how your character feels.

DISTRESS is an emotional response to extreme stress or situational triggers; it creates intense physiological results, and can affect a person's sleep patterns, eating habits, and physical and emotional reactions. Body language cues involve common self-protective mechanisms, such as: rubbing the head or nape of the neck, crossed arms (sometimes with only one arm, or as a 'self-hugging' movement), rapid breathing, pale and clammy skin, repetitive nervous movements or tics, crying, tight gripping with hands, or wide unfocused eyes.

He was still in shock, he realised. His hands wouldn't let go of the steering wheel and his breathing had ratcheted up...

_____

_____

_____

_____

_____

_____

_____

_____

_____

_____

_____

_____

_____

_____

_____

_____

_____

_____

_____

_____

_____

_____

_____

_____

_____

_____

_____

'I am neither a
man nor a woman,
but an author.'

GEORGE
ELIOT

FIVE STORY ELEMENTS

Create the missing story elements and write the story.

SITUATION _____

_____

CHARACTER A girl who disguises herself as a boy to achieve her dreams.

OPPONENT The girl's uncle, who is determined to get her back before she disgraces the family name.

GOAL
_____

_____

OBSTACLE

_____

_____

_____

_____

_____

_____

_____

_____

_____

_____

_____

_____

_____

_____

KEYWORD STORY

Include these words to write the story All in the Timing.

card	spin	red	diamond	lucky
hat	flourish	applause	knife	delicate

All in the Timing

_____
_____
_____
_____
_____
_____
_____
_____
_____
_____
_____
_____
_____
_____
_____
_____
_____
_____
_____
_____
_____
_____
_____
_____
_____
_____
_____

SETTING THE SCENE

Where does this story take place? Describe the setting as you tell the story.

When people say 'country estate', it sounds very grand. But looking at it now, I realise our house is...

_____

_____

_____

_____

_____

_____

_____

_____

_____

_____

_____

_____

_____

_____

_____

_____

_____

_____

_____

_____

_____

_____

_____

_____

_____

_____

_____

_____

_____

_____

_____

_____

_____

DIALOGUE KICKSTARTER

Write a story through dialogue alone. You can get across more than you think!

'Do we have a lock on the target?'

'Yessir, we have a lock. But, sir–'

'Prepare to fire on my orders.'

'Sir, is this... He's just a kid.'

'Are you questioning my orders, soldier?'

'No, sir. Sir, requesting more details about the target, sir.'

'... _____

_____

_____

_____

_____

_____

_____

_____

_____

_____

_____

_____

_____

_____

_____

_____

_____

_____

DON'T THINK, JUST WRITE!

Don't stop writing until you reach the bottom of the page!

What is one real historical event that you would like to write about? Explain what interests you about it.

_____

_____

_____

_____

_____

_____

_____

_____

_____

_____

_____

_____

_____

_____

_____

_____

_____

_____

_____

_____

_____

_____

_____

_____

_____

_____

STORY STARTER SENTENCE

Continue the story.

The night I set fire to Mr Wallace's barn, there was no moon at all... _____

_____

_____

_____

_____

_____

_____

_____

_____

_____

_____

_____

_____

_____

_____

_____

_____

_____

_____

_____

_____

_____

_____

_____

_____

_____

_____

_____

_____

GRAPHIC NOVEL

Use the words below in dialogue or in your drawings to create the graphic novel Magic Box.

Magic Box

assistant   glamorous   sequins   flame   hat

illusion   squeeze   mirror   audience   carefully

TRY A NEW GENRE

Have you ever written a story in this genre? Here's your chance to try something you're unfamiliar with.

PSYCHOLOGICAL THRILLER: Dropping by your boyfriend's house unexpectedly one evening, you walk into the kitchen to find him talking to his mother in a foreign language – even though he said he's never travelled and only speaks English...

_____

_____

_____

_____

_____

_____

_____

_____

_____

_____

_____

_____

_____

_____

_____

_____

_____

_____

_____

_____

_____

_____

_____

_____

_____

_____

_____

OUT-OF-CHARACTER

Write a story about a character type you know, in a situation you're not used to seeing them in.

A superhero's sidekick and a supervillain's henchman meet unexpectedly and fall for each other. How does it happen and what do they do?

_____
_____
_____
_____
_____
_____
_____
_____
_____
_____
_____
_____
_____
_____
_____
_____
_____
_____
_____
_____
_____
_____
_____
_____
_____
_____
_____
_____
_____
_____

FILL IN THE BLANK

Fill in the blanks and write the story.

He put his _____ to his mouth, until the guard told him he couldn't _____ in here.

| hand | cigarette | sandwich | whistle | laugh | eat | summon | smoke | cry |

_____

_____

_____

_____

_____

_____

_____

_____

_____

_____

_____

_____

_____

_____

_____

_____

_____

_____

_____

_____

_____

_____

_____

_____

_____

_____

_____

_____

CHARACTER CREATOR

NAME _____

OCCUPATION _____

AGE _____

SPECIAL SKILLS _____
_____

FRIENDS _____

PHYSICAL DESCRIPTION _____
_____

LIVES IN _____
_____

HOW THEY FEEL ABOUT _____
WHERE THEY LIVE _____

FAVOURITE FOOD _____

LEAST FAVOURITE FOOD _____

VICES _____
_____

MOST SIGNIFICANT _____
CHILDHOOD MEMORY _____

HANDLES BOREDOM BY _____
_____

DEALS WITH _____
FRUSTRATION BY _____

Now that you know your character, it's time to write about them.

STORY STARTER SENTENCE

Continue the story.

Every day, they met at the cliff over the roiling ocean, and every day, the ocean was the same.

Until Saturday... _____

_____

_____

_____

_____

_____

_____

_____

_____

_____

_____

_____

_____

_____

_____

_____

_____

_____

_____

_____

_____

_____

_____

_____

_____

_____

_____

_____

_____

_____

_____

_____

_____

_____

_____

KEYWORD STORY

Include these words to write the story The Incompetent Apprentice.

push	sweat	grease	iron	black
always	fingers	concentrate	garbage	irritation

The Incompetent Apprentice

_____
_____
_____
_____
_____
_____
_____
_____
_____
_____
_____
_____
_____
_____
_____
_____
_____
_____
_____
_____
_____
_____
_____
_____
_____
_____

TRY A NEW GENRE

Have you ever written a story in this genre? Here's your chance to try something you're unfamiliar with.

HORROR: Tattoos begin to spontaneously develop on your skin. You're told that the only way to find out why is to visit a notorious witch in a graveyard in the old part of town...

_____
_____
_____
_____
_____
_____
_____
_____
_____
_____
_____
_____
_____
_____
_____
_____
_____
_____
_____
_____
_____
_____
_____
_____
_____
_____
_____
_____
_____
_____

STORY STARTER SENTENCE

Continue the story.

There was a legend about the well in the woods... _____

_____

_____

_____

_____

_____

_____

_____

_____

_____

_____

_____

_____

_____

_____

_____

_____

_____

_____

_____

_____

_____

_____

_____

_____

_____

_____

_____

_____

_____

SETTING THE SCENE

Where does this story take place? Describe the setting as you tell the story.

If I'm going to be here a while, I should catalogue it: a jail cell six paces wide by ten paces long, pale grey paint on the walls... _____

_____

_____

_____

_____

_____

_____

_____

_____

_____

_____

_____

_____

_____

_____

_____

_____

_____

_____

_____

_____

_____

_____

_____

_____

_____

_____

_____

_____

_____

_____

DIALOGUE KICKSTARTER

Write a story through dialogue alone. You can get across more than you think!

'Now count four paces to the left.'

'One...two...three... four. So I dig here?'

'Is there a white rock? That's what it says, that there should be a white rock.'

'I don't see any rock. Show me the map again?'

'... _____

_____

_____

_____

_____

_____

_____

_____

_____

_____

_____

_____

_____

_____

_____

_____

_____

_____

_____

_____

_____

SECONDARY CHARACTERS

PROTAGONIST An upstart lawyer who has just been given a case that everyone considers unwinnable.

SECONDARY CHARACTER
_____
_____

PHYSICAL DESCRIPTION
_____
_____
_____
_____

PERSONALITY
_____
_____
_____
_____
_____

BACKSTORY
_____
_____
_____
_____
_____
_____
_____
_____

Fill in the secondary character profile then write a scene in which the protagonist and your secondary character interact.

_____
_____
_____
_____
_____
_____
_____

KEYWORD STORY

Include these words to write the story Black-Hearted.

flame	instinct	hawk	dusk	thoughtful
squint	sardonic	teeth	swift	hollow

Black-Hearted

_____
_____
_____
_____
_____
_____
_____
_____
_____
_____
_____
_____
_____
_____
_____
_____
_____
_____
_____
_____
_____
_____
_____
_____
_____
_____
_____
_____
_____

DON'T THINK, JUST WRITE!

Write down all the things that you feel readers don't see enough of in stories.

_____
_____
_____
_____
_____
_____
_____
_____
_____
_____
_____
_____
_____
_____
_____
_____
_____
_____
_____
_____
_____
_____
_____
_____
_____
_____
_____
_____
_____
_____
_____

FIVE STORY ELEMENTS

Create the missing story elements and write the story.

SITUATION   The son of a dangerous crime boss makes a connection with the daughter of a renowned FBI agent.

CHARACTER   _____
              _____

OPPONENT   _____
              _____

GOAL   _____
              _____

OBSTACLE
              _____
              _____

_____
_____
_____
_____
_____
_____
_____
_____
_____
_____
_____
_____
_____
_____
_____

GRAPHIC NOVEL

Use the words below in dialogue or in your drawings to create the graphic novel Thin Air.

Thin Air

altitude	climbing	crampons	rope	snow
slide	pack	gasp	gloves	black

SECONDARY CHARACTERS

PROTAGONIST   The primary dancer in a major ballet company, who suffers from crippling shyness.

SECONDARY CHARACTER   _____

_____

PHYSICAL DESCRIPTION   _____

_____

_____

PERSONALITY   _____

_____

_____

_____

_____

BACKSTORY   _____

_____

_____

_____

_____

_____

_____

_____

Fill in the secondary character profile then write a scene in which the protagonist and your secondary character interact.

_____

_____

_____

_____

_____

_____

_____

SETTING THE SCENE

Where does this story take place? Describe the setting as you tell the story.

The inside of the car was unsanitary. There were hamburger wrappers in the footwell, chewing gum

on the dash... _____

_____

_____

_____

_____

_____

_____

_____

_____

_____

_____

_____

_____

_____

_____

_____

_____

_____

_____

_____

_____

_____

_____

_____

_____

_____

_____

_____

_____

STORY STARTER SENTENCE

Continue the story.

I've tied the last knot in the bedsheets; I can only hope they hold. When I throw the window open and toss my sheet-line out, the night is cool and quiet... _____

_____

_____

_____

_____

_____

_____

_____

_____

_____

_____

_____

_____

_____

_____

_____

_____

_____

_____

_____

_____

_____

_____

_____

_____

_____

_____

_____

_____

_____

_____

_____

CHARACTER CREATOR

NAME _____

OCCUPATION _____

AGE _____

SPECIAL SKILLS _____
_____

FRIENDS _____

PHYSICAL DESCRIPTION _____
_____

LIVES IN _____
_____

HOW THEY FEEL ABOUT
WHERE THEY LIVE _____
_____

FAVOURITE FOOD _____

LEAST FAVOURITE FOOD _____

VICES _____
_____

MOST SIGNIFICANT
CHILDHOOD MEMORY _____
_____

HANDLES BOREDOM BY _____
_____

DEALS WITH
FRUSTRATION BY _____
_____

Now that you know your character, it's time to write about them.

_____

_____

_____

_____

_____

_____

_____

_____

_____

_____

_____

_____

_____

_____

_____

_____

_____

_____

_____

_____

_____

_____

_____

_____

_____

_____

_____

_____

_____

_____

_____

TRY A NEW GENRE

Have you ever written a story in this genre? Here's your chance to try something you're unfamiliar with.

HISTORICAL ROMANCE: A princess who has been promised in marriage to a neighbouring king's son decides to escape her fate. But when she reaches the stables to quietly saddle her horse, she bumps into the king's son, who is quietly saddling his horse...

_____

_____

_____

_____

_____

_____

_____

_____

_____

_____

_____

_____

_____

_____

_____

_____

_____

_____

_____

_____

_____

_____

_____

_____

_____

_____

_____

_____

_____

OUT-OF-CHARACTER

Write a story about a character type you know, in a situation you're not used to seeing them in.

Death gets tired of gloom and doom and decides to go on a beach holiday. What happens when Death goes to visit the travel agent?

_____

_____

_____

_____

_____

_____

_____

_____

_____

_____

_____

_____

_____

_____

_____

_____

_____

_____

_____

_____

_____

_____

_____

_____

_____

_____

_____

_____

_____